Servicepreneurship:

Launch Your Profitable Service Business with Confidence

PETERSON HERARD

Table of Contents

Foreword

The year was 2019 when I had the privilege of welcoming a driven and tenacious individual into my coaching program: Peterson Herard. Throughout our interactions, Peterson's unwavering commitment to both personal and professional growth resonated deeply with me. Today, as I pen down this forward, I am filled with an overwhelming sense of pride and admiration for the journey he has undertaken.

It isn't common to come across individuals who genuinely exemplify the perfect blend of ambition and integrity. Peterson is that rarity. Grounded in his Christian faith, he brings a unique blend of ethical business practices to the table, emphasizing the significance of not just being successful but also being impactful. And as a testament to his character, Peterson stands tall not just as a businessman but as a devoted husband and a loving father. It's this holistic approach to life that sets him apart, ensuring he shines not just in one, but every aspect of life.

I was honored when Peterson spoke at one of my mastermind events. The audience was captivated, hanging onto every word, as he effortlessly shared his insights, experiences, and actionable strategies. It was evident that here was a man who wasn't just knowledgeable but genuinely passionate about helping others achieve their dreams.

And now, Peterson has taken his wisdom, expertise, and passion and encapsulated it in Servicepreneurship: Launch Your Profitable Service Business with Confidence. This book isn't just another guide; it's a masterclass for those who dream of turning their passion into a thriving service business. The strategies, practical tips, and proven techniques that Peterson shares in these pages are the result of his dedication, his mistakes, his learnings, and his triumphs.

To every reader, I have a simple message: you're about to embark on a transformative journey. As you delve into the depths of Servicepreneurship, be prepared to be inspired, enlightened, and above all, empowered. This isn't just a book; it's a roadmap for success, meticulously crafted by someone who has traversed the path, faced its challenges, and emerged victoriously.

In recommending Peterson's book, I am not just endorsing its content but celebrating its author, his ethos, and the unparalleled value he brings to the entrepreneurial realm. If there's anyone equipped to guide you towards launching your service business with confidence and making it exceptionally profitable, it's Peterson Herard.

Embrace the journey. Let Peterson be your guide. The horizon of success awaits you.
Many Blessings,
Jacob Salem

Preface

Welcome to Servicepreneurship: Launch Your Profitable Service Business with Confidence. I am honored to share my personal journey and experiences with you, as someone who has navigated the trials and triumphs of entrepreneurship in the service industry.

My story begins in the banking industry, where I had the privilege of working for esteemed companies such as JPMorgan Chase Bank, Northern Trust, and Florida Community Bank. After Synovus Bank acquired Florida Community Bank, I made the bold decision to step down from my managerial position and transition into a senior banker role. Little did I know that this change would ultimately lead me down a path of entrepreneurship and service-based ventures.

Just when life seemed to be settling into a comfortable routine, an unexpected event altered the course of my career. My wife gave birth to our beautiful daughter, and in that moment, my priorities shifted. I realized that I wanted more than just a stable job; I wanted the freedom to spend quality time with my family while pursuing my passion for financial services.

Without a backup plan and filled with equal parts fear and determination, I took a leap of faith and embarked on a freelancing journey. Utilizing my expertise in finance, I began assisting individuals and companies with their financial needs while simultaneously delving into the world of marketing. It was during this time that fate intervened, as I had the privilege of crossing paths with a remarkable individual named Jacob Salem.

Under Jacob's guidance and through my certification with his esteemed company EZMetrics, I became a certified digital marketer. With newfound knowledge and a growing client base, I took a decisive step forward and founded my first service company, Reap and Sow Media, in 2019. Specializing in digital marketing services for lawyers, professional service businesses, and local enterprises, I poured my heart and soul into building a successful venture.

Through relentless dedication and unwavering commitment to delivering exceptional results, Reap and Sow Media quickly surpassed expectations, propelling my company to surpass multiple six-figure earnings within the span of just one year. It was through this remarkable journey that I discovered my true calling—a mission to help ambitious professionals like yourself launch and grow service-based businesses, whether on a part-time or full-time basis.

In "Servicepreneurship: Launch Your Profitable Service Business with Confidence," I draw upon my firsthand experiences, the lessons learned, and the strategies that have proven successful in my own entrepreneurial endeavors. It is my sincerest desire to impart this knowledge and provide you with the necessary tools, insights, and confidence to embark on your own servicepreneurship journey.

Whether you are a seasoned professional seeking a new venture or an aspiring entrepreneur with a dream, this book will equip you with practical advice, real-world examples, and actionable strategies to guide you through every step of the process. Together, we will unlock the potential of your service business and transform your aspirations into a thriving reality.

I am honored to join you on this transformative journey. Let us embark on this path of servicepreneurship, where dreams are nurtured, businesses flourish, and ambitious professionals like yourself achieve remarkable success. I eagerly await witnessing the impact you will make in the service industry.

Introduction

In a world of relentless change and endless possibilities, the concept of work and entrepreneurship has undergone a transformation like never before. The traditional 9-to-5 grind is no longer the only path to financial success, personal fulfillment, and the freedom to shape your destiny. Today, a new breed of entrepreneurs is emerging—one that is driven not only by profits but also by purpose, not just by ambition but also by a burning desire to serve.

Welcome to "Servicepreneurship: Launch Your Profitable Service Business with Confidence." This book is your roadmap to unlocking the boundless potential within you and harnessing your existing skills to embark on an entrepreneurial journey like no other. It's a journey that promises not only financial rewards but also the satisfaction of making a real difference in the lives of your clients and customers.

The world of service-based entrepreneurship is a realm where your passion, expertise, and commitment can flourish, where you can transform your knowledge into a thriving business that not only sustains you but also empowers you to live life on your own terms.

Are you an ambitious professional who's been dreaming of breaking free from the corporate treadmill? Perhaps you're tired of the monotony of your 9-to-5 job, the limited earning potential, or the feeling that you're just a small cog in a big machine. Or maybe you're just yearning for a more flexible lifestyle, one where you can prioritize your family, passions, and personal growth while still achieving financial success.

If any of these resonate with you, you're not alone. The rise of the servicepreneur is a global phenomenon—a testament to the human spirit's innate desire for autonomy, creativity, and a purpose-driven life. And the best part? You don't need to reinvent the wheel or start from scratch. You have a powerful asset already within you—your skills and expertise.

In the pages that follow, we will dive deep into the world of Servicepreneurship, exploring the art and science of turning your skills into a profitable service business. Whether you're a consultant, freelancer, coach, designer, writer, programmer, or possess any specialized knowledge, you hold the key to your entrepreneurial destiny.

Servicepreneurship is not just about building a business; it's about building a life that you love. It's about designing your own future, setting your own rules, and creating a legacy that transcends mere financial success. This book will equip you with the knowledge, strategies, and mindset required to launch your service business with confidence, whether you're looking to start part-time or dive in full-time.

The journey to Servicepreneurship may not always be easy, but it's undoubtedly one of the most rewarding paths you can choose.

It's a journey where you'll grow not only as an entrepreneur but also as a person, as you learn to overcome obstacles, embrace uncertainty, and find fulfillment in the pursuit of your dreams.

So, are you ready to take the first step toward a life of purpose, autonomy, and financial prosperity? Are you prepared to harness your skills and talents to create a thriving service business that serves both you and your clients? If your answer is a resounding "yes," then let's embark on this transformative journey together. Your servicepreneurial adventure begins now, and I'm here to guide you every step of the way.

The Importance of Service Businesses

Service businesses play a vital role in today's economy, providing a range of valuable services that meet the needs and wants of customers. These businesses differ from traditional product-based businesses, as they primarily focus on delivering intangible services rather than tangible goods. Understanding the importance of service businesses is crucial for entrepreneurs looking to launch and grow their service-based ventures.

One key advantage of service businesses is the opportunity for customization and personalization. Unlike physical products, services are highly adaptable and can be tailored to meet the specific requirements of individual customers. For example, a consulting firm can provide personalized advice and recommendations based on a client's unique circumstances and goals. This level of customization allows service businesses to create a more personalized and enjoyable experience for their customers, fostering customer loyalty and repeat business.

Moreover, service businesses are often characterized by higher profit margins compared to product-based businesses. The cost of producing services is relatively low as they do not involve the expenses associated with manufacturing, inventory management, and distribution. As a result, service businesses can generate higher profits while minimizing overhead costs. For instance, an online tutoring service may require minimal infrastructure and can scale its operations more easily and cost-effectively compared to a physical tutoring center.

Additionally, service businesses play a significant role in employment and job creation. According to the International Labor Organization, the service sector is the largest employer worldwide, accounting for approximately 60% of global employment. Service businesses offer diverse job opportunities and can contribute to economic growth by providing employment opportunities across various skill levels. For instance, a digital marketing agency may employ marketing specialists, content creators, designers, and project managers, creating job opportunities for individuals with different expertise.

Furthermore, service businesses contribute to the overall well-being and development of societies by addressing essential needs and improving the quality of life. Healthcare services, for example, are crucial for the well-being of individuals and communities, providing medical care, preventive measures, and wellness programs. Educational services play an integral role in shaping the future workforce by providing knowledge and skills necessary for personal and professional growth. By providing these vital services, service businesses contribute to the overall prosperity and development of communities.

Overall, service businesses are important due to their ability to provide customized solutions, higher profit potential, job creation, and their impact on social and economic development. Entrepreneurs who recognize the value and potential of service businesses can capitalize on these advantages and build successful ventures that meet the evolving needs of customers and contribute to a prosperous society.

The Servicepreneur Mindset

The Servicepreneur Mindset is a crucial aspect of launching and growing a successful service-based business. It encompasses the attitudes, beliefs, and mindset that service entrepreneurs need to develop to overcome challenges, take risks, and ultimately achieve their goals. Adopting a Servicepreneur Mindset is essential for building confidence and resilience, as well as for developing the necessary skills and strategies to navigate the competitive landscape of the service industry.

One key element of the Servicepreneur Mindset is a strong customer-centric focus. Servicepreneurs understand that their success depends on delivering exceptional customer service and meeting the needs of their clients. They prioritize understanding their customers' pain points, preferences, and expectations and seek to provide tailored solutions that exceed their clients' expectations. By putting the customer at the center of their business, servicepreneurs can build strong relationships, foster customer loyalty, and generate positive word-of-mouth referrals.

Another important aspect of the Servicepreneur Mindset is a willingness to continuously learn and adapt. Service businesses operate in dynamic and ever-changing environments, and servicepreneurs must stay updated on industry trends, technological advancements, and best practices to remain competitive. They actively seek out new knowledge and skills to improve their service offerings, stay ahead of the competition, and identify new opportunities for growth. Adopting a growth mindset and being open to feedback and new ideas are key traits of successful servicepreneurs.

Additionally, servicepreneurs possess an entrepreneurial mindset, which involves taking calculated risks and embracing innovation. They are not afraid to step outside their comfort zones, try new approaches, and explore unconventional solutions to meet customer needs. Servicepreneurs understand that taking risks is a necessary part of growth and that failure is an opportunity for learning and improvement. They are resilient in the face of challenges and setbacks and persevere in their pursuit of business success.

To cultivate the Servicepreneur Mindset, aspiring servicepreneurs can engage in activities such as reading books and articles on entrepreneurship and self-improvement, attending seminars and workshops, and surrounding themselves with like-minded individuals who support their goals.

By developing a service-oriented mindset, entrepreneurs can build a strong foundation for their service businesses and set themselves up for long-term success.

Here are two Examples:

A well-known example of the servicepreneur mindset is that of Richard Branson, founder of Virgin Group. Branson is known for his relentless focus on customer satisfaction and his ability to create innovative and customer-centered solutions. He consistently seeks feedback from customers and uses it to improve his business offerings. Branson's success can be attributed in part to his strong servicepreneur mindset and his dedication to providing exceptional service.

Another example is Airbnb, a groundbreaking service-based business that disrupted the hospitality industry. The founders of Airbnb adopted a servicepreneur mindset by recognizing the unmet needs of travelers and hosts alike and creating a platform that connected them. They took a risk by opening up their own homes to strangers, and their servicepreneur mindset allowed them to build trust, adapt to changing customer preferences, and ultimately become a dominant player in the travel industry.

Identifying Your Service Business Idea

Identifying a strong and viable service business idea is the first crucial step in launching a profitable service-based business. Your business idea should not only align with your skills and interests but also address a specific need or problem in the market. This section will guide you through the process of identifying and evaluating potential service business ideas.

To begin, brainstorm a list of potential service business ideas that you are passionate about and that align with your expertise. Consider your professional background, skills, and experiences, as these can serve as a strong foundation for your business idea.

For example, if you have a background in graphic design, you could consider starting a graphic design agency, offering design services to clients.

If you have a background in photography, you could consider starting a photography studio, offering professional photography services for events and portraits.

If you have experience in fitness and wellness, you could consider starting a personal training business, offering customized workout plans and nutrition guidance to clients.

If you have expertise in social media marketing, you could consider starting a digital marketing agency, offering social media management and advertising services to businesses.

If you have a background in writing and editing, you could consider starting a freelance writing business, offering content creation and proofreading services to individuals and businesses.

If you have a passion for event planning, you could consider starting an event management company, offering full-service event planning and coordination for weddings, corporate events, and parties.

If you have knowledge and skills in home organization, you could consider starting a professional organizing service, helping clients declutter and create organized living spaces.

If you have a background in software development, you could consider starting a software consulting firm, offering custom software solutions and technical support to businesses.

If you have expertise in financial planning and investment, you could consider starting a financial advisory business, providing personalized financial advice and investment strategies to individuals and families.

If you have a passion for baking and culinary arts, you could consider starting a specialty bakery, offering customized cakes and pastries for weddings, birthdays, and special occasions.

If you have experience in eco-friendly practices, you could consider starting a sustainable consulting business, helping companies implement environmentally friendly initiatives and practices.

Once you have brainstormed your initial list of ideas, it is essential to validate them by conducting market research. This research will help you determine the demand for your services and evaluate the competition in the market. Start by identifying your target market and understanding their needs and preferences. This can be done through surveys, focus groups, or analyzing existing market data.

Additionally, conduct a competitor analysis to evaluate the existing service providers in your chosen market. Look for gaps or opportunities where you can differentiate yourself from the competition. For example, if you want to start a food delivery service in a crowded market, you could differentiate yourself by offering specialized healthy meal options for specific dietary requirements.

Market trends and opportunities should also be considered when identifying your service business idea. Stay updated on industry news, emerging technologies, and changing customer preferences. For example, the rise of remote work and virtual events presents an opportunity for service businesses that cater to remote workers or provide virtual event management services.

It is crucial to thoroughly research and evaluate each potential business idea to ensure its profitability and sustainability. Consider factors such as the market demand, competition, scalability, and cost-effectiveness. This evaluation process will help you narrow down your list and choose the most promising service business idea.

Remember, choosing the right service business idea requires careful consideration and research. By identifying a niche or addressing an unmet need in the market, you can position yourself for success and stand out from the competition. This process will set the foundation for your service-based business and give you the confidence to move forward with your entrepreneurial journey.

Understanding your target market

Understanding your target market is indeed the crucial and most important part of building a successful service business. It is important to remember that people do not just buy a service; they buy a solution to their problem or a way to achieve their desired outcome. Therefore, it is crucial for servicepreneurs to deeply understand the pain points and challenges that their target market is facing. By doing so, they can position their service as the bridge and the solution that helps their target market achieve their desired solution.

For example, let's consider the target market of a fitness coach who specializes in weight loss for busy professionals. The fitness coach understands that their target market, busy professionals, often struggle with finding time to exercise and maintain a healthy lifestyle due to their hectic work schedules. By understanding this pain point, the fitness coach can design their service in a way that specifically addresses this challenge. They can offer convenient online workout programs or personalized training sessions that can be easily integrated into the busy professional's daily routine. This way, the fitness coach's service becomes the solution that helps busy professionals achieve their weight loss goals despite their limited time.

Another example is a marketing consultant who targets small businesses in the fashion industry. The marketing consultant understands that small businesses in this industry often struggle with building brand awareness and attracting customers in a competitive market. By understanding this pain point, the marketing consultant can offer specialized marketing strategies and techniques tailored to the unique needs of the fashion industry. They can provide services such as social media marketing campaigns, influencer collaborations, and targeted advertising to help fashion businesses overcome their challenges and stand out in the market.

In both of these examples, the understanding of the target market's pain points and challenges allows the servicepreneurs to design their services in a way that directly addresses those needs. This not only helps them attract and retain their target market but also positions them as the go-to solution provider in their respective industries.

Therefore, servicepreneurs should invest time and effort in thoroughly understanding their target market's needs, preferences, and pain points. This can be done through market research, surveys, focus groups, and direct customer interactions. By gaining deep insights into their target market, servicepreneurs can create services that not only meet the demands effectively but also provide a compelling and valuable solution to their customers' problems.

Here are a couple of effective ways for servicepreneurs to understand their target market:

Direct Communication: The best way to understand the pain points and challenges of the target market is by communicating directly with potential customers. This can be done through one-on-one interviews, focus groups, or even casual conversations. By engaging in open and honest discussions, servicepreneurs can gain firsthand knowledge of their target market's needs, preferences, and pain points. It is important to ask relevant questions and actively listen to their responses to truly understand their problems and challenges. Remember, never assume you know what the pain point is or assume that you know the problem your target market is facing. Always do research and confirm.

Market Research: Conducting market research is another effective way to gather valuable insights about the target market. This can include analyzing existing data, such as industry reports, competitor analysis, and customer feedback. Servicepreneurs can also utilize various research methods, such as surveys, questionnaires, and online polls, to collect quantitative and qualitative data. By analyzing this data, servicepreneurs can identify trends, patterns, and common pain points of their target market. This information can then be used to shape their service offerings and marketing strategies more effectively.

Again, it is important for servicepreneurs to remember that understanding the target market is an ongoing process. As market dynamics change and customer needs evolve, continuous research and communication with the target market become crucial. By staying in touch with their customers and constantly evaluating their needs, servicepreneurs can ensure that their service remains relevant and continues to provide the desired solution.

Market Trends and Opportunities

Market trends and opportunities play a crucial role in the success of a service business. By staying abreast of current trends and identifying emerging opportunities, servicepreneurs can position themselves for growth and profitability. In this section, we will explore some key market trends and opportunities that servicepreneurs should consider when starting or expanding their businesses.

One market trend that has gained significant momentum in recent years is the shift towards remote work and virtual services. With advancements in technology and an increasing number of businesses adopting flexible work arrangements, there has been a growing demand for virtual service providers. This presents an opportunity for servicepreneurs to offer services such as virtual assistance, online consulting, and remote project management. By tapping into this trend, servicepreneurs can reach a broader client base and expand their business without geographical limitations.

Another market trend is the increasing emphasis on sustainability and eco-friendly practices. Consumers are becoming more conscious of their environmental footprint and are actively seeking service providers that prioritize sustainability. Servicepreneurs can capitalize on this trend by incorporating eco-friendly practices into their operations. For example, a cleaning service could use environmentally friendly cleaning products, or a consulting firm could offer sustainability audits to help businesses become more eco-friendly. By aligning their business with this trend, servicepreneurs can attract environmentally conscious clients and differentiate themselves from competitors.

Furthermore, the rise of social media and digital marketing has opened up new opportunities for service-based businesses to reach and engage their target audience. Platforms like Facebook, Instagram, and LinkedIn allow servicepreneurs to showcase their expertise, build a strong online presence, and connect with potential clients. By leveraging social media marketing strategies, servicepreneurs can increase brand visibility, generate leads, and drive traffic to their website. Additionally, online advertising platforms like Google Ads and Facebook Ads enable servicepreneurs to target their ideal customers with precision, maximizing the return on their marketing investment.

To identify market trends and opportunities, servicepreneurs should conduct thorough market research and analysis. This involves gathering data on customer preferences, industry trends, and competitor offerings. Various online resources and tools can aid servicepreneurs in this process. For instance, industry reports and market research studies provide valuable insights into market dynamics and consumer behavior. Additionally, online platforms like Google Trends and social media monitoring tools allow servicepreneurs to track popular topics and conversations related to their industry. By utilizing these resources, servicepreneurs can develop a deeper understanding of their target market and identify potential niches or gaps within the market.

Overall, staying informed about market trends and identifying opportunities is essential for the success of a service-based business. By recognizing and adapting to emerging trends, servicepreneurs can stay ahead of the competition and position themselves as industry leaders. Whether it's leveraging remote work opportunities, embracing sustainability, or utilizing digital marketing platforms, servicepreneurs can capitalize on market trends to drive growth and profitability.

Focusing on what really matters

One common observation in the world of servicepreneurship is that many service-based business owners often dedicate significant time and energy to aspects that may not have a direct impact on their success. It is not uncommon to see servicepreneurs constantly redesigning their websites, changing their logos, and engaging in other similar activities that may not truly matter in the grand scheme of things.

While having a visually appealing website and an eye-catching logo are undoubtedly important elements of your brand identity, it is crucial to remember that these external factors do not hold as much weight in the eyes of your clients. Ultimately, what clients truly care about is whether you can deliver results and effectively solve their pain points.

In the competitive landscape of service-oriented businesses, your ability to meet the needs and desires of your target audience exceeds the importance of any superficial changes to your website or logo. Clients prioritize tangible outcomes and the resolution of their challenges over aesthetics alone.

Therefore, as a servicepreneur, it is essential to focus your time and resources on activities that directly contribute to delivering exceptional results to your clients. This means honing your skills, constantly improving your service delivery process, and enhancing your problem-solving abilities.

While maintaining a visually appealing brand identity can elevate your professionalism and credibility, it is crucial to strike a balance between investing in these external aspects and continuously striving to excel in your core services. Your clients will ultimately judge your business based on the value you bring to their lives, the solutions you provide, and your consistent ability to address their pain points.

By prioritizing the quality of your service and consistently exceeding client expectations, you will build a strong reputation in the industry. Remember, your brand's reputation is forged not only through logos and websites but by consistently demonstrating your capability to deliver exceptional results and provide effective solutions to your clients' problems.

While having a visually appealing website and an eye-catching logo are undoubtedly important elements of your brand identity, it is crucial to remember that these external factors do not hold as much weight in the eyes of your clients. Ultimately, what clients truly care about is whether you can deliver results and effectively solve their pain points.

In the competitive landscape of service-oriented businesses, your ability to meet the needs and desires of your target audience exceeds the importance of any superficial changes to your website or logo. Clients prioritize tangible outcomes and the resolution of their challenges over aesthetics alone.

Therefore, as a servicepreneur, it is essential to focus your time and resources on activities that directly contribute to delivering exceptional results to your clients. This means honing your skills, constantly improving your service delivery process, and enhancing your problem-solving abilities.

While maintaining a visually appealing brand identity can elevate your professionalism and credibility, it is crucial to strike a balance between investing in these external aspects and continuously striving to excel in your core services. Your clients will ultimately judge your business based on the value you bring to their lives, the solutions you provide, and your consistent ability to address their pain points.

By prioritizing the quality of your service and consistently exceeding client expectations, you will build a strong reputation in the industry. Remember, your brand's reputation is forged not only through logos and websites but by consistently demonstrating your capability to deliver exceptional results and provide effective solutions to your clients' problems.

Case Studies: Successful Service-Based Businesses

Studying the success stories of established service-based businesses can provide valuable insights and inspiration for aspiring servicepreneurs. In this section, we will explore a few case studies of successful service-based businesses and highlight the strategies that contributed to their growth and profitability.

1. Airbnb: Disrupting the Hospitality Industry

Airbnb is a prime example of a service-based business that disrupted an entire industry. Founded in 2008, Airbnb transformed the way people travel and find accommodations. By offering a platform that connects travelers with unique lodging options provided by individual hosts, Airbnb tapped into the sharing economy and provided a more personalized and cost-effective alternative to traditional hotels.

Key Strategies:

User-Centric Experience: Airbnb focused on creating a seamless and user-friendly experience for both hosts and guests. The platform allowed hosts to showcase their properties through detailed listings and high-quality photos, while guests could browse and book accommodations that suited their preferences and budget.

Trust and Safety: Airbnb implemented measures to ensure trust and safety within its community. This included user verification, secure payment processing, and reviews from both hosts and guests. By prioritizing safety, Airbnb built credibility and encouraged users to engage with the platform.

Community Building: Airbnb fostered a sense of community among hosts and guests by encouraging interactions and providing resources for hosts to enhance their listings. This community-driven approach created a loyal user base and promoted positive word-of-mouth marketing.

2. Upwork: Empowering Freelancers and Businesses

Upwork is a leading online platform that connects freelancers with businesses seeking various services, from writing and design to programming and marketing. Founded in 2015 through the merger of odes and Elance, Upwork revolutionized the way businesses find talent and how freelancers access opportunities.

Key Strategies:

Diverse Talent Pool: Upwork created a vast and diverse marketplace of freelancers with various skills and expertise. This allowed businesses to find the right professionals for their projects, while freelancers could access a wide range of job opportunities.

Flexible Engagement: Upwork enabled businesses to hire freelancers for short-term projects, long-term contracts, or even hourly work. This flexibility catered to the changing needs of businesses and provided freelancers with diverse income streams.

Secure Transactions: Upwork implemented a secure payment system that guaranteed freelancers' compensation and protected clients' payments. This built trust between parties and eliminated concerns about payment disputes.

3. HelloFresh: Revolutionizing Meal Delivery

HelloFresh is a meal kit delivery service that provides customers with pre-portioned ingredients and recipes to prepare meals at home. Founded in 2011, HelloFresh transformed the way people approach cooking by offering convenience, variety, and flexibility.

Key Strategies:

Convenience and Simplification: HelloFresh addressed the challenge of meal planning and grocery shopping by providing pre-selected ingredients and step-by-step recipes. This simplified the cooking process and offered busy individuals a convenient solution for home-cooked meals.

Customization: HelloFresh allowed customers to choose from a variety of meal options based on dietary preferences, family size, and taste preferences. This customization catered to a broad audience and ensured customer satisfaction.

Quality Ingredients: HelloFresh emphasized the use of high-quality, fresh ingredients in its meal kits. By delivering fresh produce and premium ingredients, HelloFresh provided value and elevated the cooking experience.

These case studies showcase how successful service-based businesses identified market needs, addressed pain points, and leveraged innovative approaches to create valuable solutions for their customers. By adopting user-centric approaches, building trust, and embracing innovation, these businesses achieved remarkable growth and established themselves as leaders in their respective industries.

Understanding the landscape of service entrepreneurship, identifying market trends and opportunities, and focusing on delivering exceptional value are key factors that contribute to the success of a service-based business. By adopting the Servicepreneur Mindset and prioritizing the needs of your target market, you can navigate the challenges of entrepreneurship with confidence and build a profitable service business.

Developing Your Service Offerings

Creating compelling and valuable service offerings is a crucial aspect of building a profitable service-based business. In the next few chapters, we will explore the different strategies and considerations involved in developing services that meet the needs and preferences of your target market. By understanding how to design your service portfolio, price your offerings appropriately, choose the right service delivery models, and prioritize customer satisfaction, you can position your business for success and stand out from the competition.

To begin, we will delve into the process of designing your service portfolio. This involves identifying the specific services you will offer, determining their scope and features, and ensuring they align with the unique value proposition of your business. We will discuss how to conduct market research and gather customer insights to determine which services are in demand and how to tailor them to meet the specific needs and preferences of your target market.

Next, we will explore pricing strategies for service businesses. Pricing can be a complex and critical aspect of service offerings, as it directly affects profitability and perceived value. We will cover various pricing models and techniques, such as tiered pricing, value-based pricing, and subscription-based pricing, to help you determine the most effective approach for your business.

Additionally, we will discuss different service delivery models, including in-person services, online services, and hybrid models. Choosing the right delivery model is essential to ensure efficient and effective service provision, as well as meeting the expectations of your customers. We will examine the advantages and challenges of each model and provide guidance on how to select the most suitable option for your business.

Finally, customer satisfaction is paramount in service-based businesses. We will explore strategies for delivering high-quality services, exceeding customer expectations, and maintaining long-term customer relationships. By prioritizing customer satisfaction and utilizing feedback mechanisms, you can continuously improve your service offerings and build a loyal customer base.

I will equip you with the knowledge and tools to develop service offerings that resonate with your target market and drive business growth. By focusing on creating valuable and differentiated services, pricing them effectively, choosing the right delivery models, and prioritizing customer satisfaction, you will be well-prepared to maximize the success and profitability of your service-based business.

The Importance of Expertise in Servicepreneurship part 1

In the world of servicepreneurship, being an expert in your field is crucial for attracting and retaining clients. This chapter explores the significance of expertise in service businesses and highlights the advantages of being a specialist rather than a generalist.

1. Confused Buyers Never Buy

The saying "confused buyers never buy" emphasizes the importance of clarity in your service offerings. When potential clients are unsure about how you can help them, they are less likely to make a purchase. By being an expert in your field, you can clearly communicate the value and benefits you provide, making it easier for clients to understand and engage with your services.

2. The Power of Specialization

Being a generalist may seem appealing, as it allows you to offer a wide range of services. However, specialization has its own set of advantages. When you focus on a specific niche or industry, you can develop a deep understanding of your clients' needs and challenges. This expertise allows you to tailor your services to meet their specific requirements, making you more valuable and sought after.

3. The Perception of Value

Clients perceive experts as highly skilled professionals who possess in-depth knowledge and experience in their field. This perception of value often leads to clients being willing to pay premium prices for specialized services. By positioning yourself as an expert, you can command higher rates, increasing your profitability and overall success.

4. Building Trust and Credibility

Expertise builds trust and credibility with potential clients. When you can showcase your knowledge and success in solving specific problems, clients are more likely to trust your abilities to deliver results. Including case studies, testimonials, or examples of past successful projects in your service portfolio can strengthen your credibility and help you win the trust of potential clients.

5. Continuous Learning and Improvement

As an expert, it is crucial to continuously update your skills and knowledge to stay ahead in the industry. By investing in ongoing learning and professional development, you can offer the latest and most effective solutions to your clients. Continuously refining and enhancing your services ensure that you remain competitive and meet the evolving needs of your target market.

6. Being a Trusted Advisor

By positioning yourself as an expert, you can go beyond being a service provider and become a trusted advisor to your clients. Clients often seek guidance and direction from experts in their field, and by establishing yourself as a thought leader, you can provide valuable insights and recommendations. This not only strengthens your client relationships but also allows you to cross-sell and upsell additional services.

The Importance of Expertise in Servicepreneurship part 2

The rule of one, as I call it, is a fundamental principle that servicepreneurs must embrace to achieve success in their businesses. It revolves around the idea of becoming an expert and authority in a specific niche. By focusing on one service and one niche, servicepreneurs can position themselves as the go-to resource for individuals or businesses seeking solutions within that particular area.

To better understand the rule of one, let's consider a medical analogy. When someone falls ill, they typically visit a general family doctor who can provide a broad range of medical assistance. However, if someone were to break their foot, they would be better served by seeing a podiatrist, a specialist solely focused on foot-related conditions. Although the fee charged by the podiatrist may be higher compared to the general doctor, the specialized knowledge and expertise they possess result in a higher quality of service and a greater likelihood of effective treatment.

Similarly, servicepreneurs who offer a wide range of services or try to cater to a broad audience run the risk of diluting their expertise and not being able to deliver exceptional value. By narrowing their focus to one specific service and specializing in a particular niche, servicepreneurs increase their chances of becoming recognized authorities in their field. This specialization allows them to stand out from their competition and attract clients who specifically seek their niche expertise.

By honing their skills and dedicating themselves to a particular service and niche, servicepreneurs cultivate a reputation as experts in their field. This expertise not only enhances their credibility but also enables them to command higher prices for their specialized services. Clients value the specialized knowledge, experience, and insights that servicepreneurs bring to the table, which translates into a willingness to pay a premium for their expertise.

Once a servicepreneur has established themselves as an authority in their niche and successfully delivered their service to a client, there is an opportunity to explore additional avenues. After a client is satisfied with the initial service rendered, servicepreneurs can consider cross-selling and upselling complementary services. This approach is effective because the client has already experienced the high quality of service provided and trusts the expertise of the servicepreneur. By expanding their offerings strategically, servicepreneurs can capitalize on the trust and satisfaction built with their clients, further enhancing their business growth and profitability.

In summary, the rule of one emphasizes the significance of specialization and niche expertise in the world of servicepreneurship. By focusing on one service and one target market, servicepreneurs can establish themselves as experts, attract clients who value their specialized knowledge, and ultimately drive business growth and profitability. Embracing the rule of one allows servicepreneurs to differentiate themselves from the competition and position themselves as trusted authorities in their chosen niche.

Creating an irresistible offer

When creating an offer for your customers, it is important to understand that it goes beyond a simple sales promotion. An offer is a well-crafted solution that is highly beneficial to the customer and something they cannot resist. The value of the offer should exceed its cost, making it a "no-brainer" for the customer.

To create an offer that is tailored to your customers, you need to identify their biggest pain points. Start by focusing on what they need and address their specific problems. For instance, if you are a business consultant, your target audience may struggle with low interest in product launches, lack of traffic, or struggling to increase ROI. Choose one pain point to focus on and position yourself as an expert in that area.

For example, if you choose "low interest in product launches" as the pain point, you can create a package that supports businesses in planning a product launch relevant to their target audience.

This package may include customer research with surveys and polls, testing product labels/packaging, marketing support for the launch, creating measurable goals, advertising strategies, and campaigns for generating excitement, sales, and follow-up.

Your offer needs to be holistic and provide an immediate solution to your customer's problem. Give your package a compelling name that reflects its benefits, such as "Guaranteed Higher Interest in Your Product Launch". This name should catch the customer's attention and make them eager to learn more about the offer.

it is also important to consider the customer's level of awareness when promoting your offer. There are five levels of awareness: unaware, problem aware, solution aware, product aware, and most aware. The customer's level of awareness will determine the type of information you provide them and whether they are ready to commit to your offer.

Ensure that your offer is relevant to the customer's specific stage of awareness. If they are unaware of the problem or your solution, you need to educate them about the benefits of your offer. If they are problem aware, emphasize how your offer can solve their specific problem. As they become more solution aware or product aware, provide more details about your offer and convince them that it is the right solution for them. Ultimately, your goal is to reach the "most aware" stage where the customer knows about your product, understands its value, and wants to purchase it.

By understanding your customer's pain points and creating a compelling offer that addresses those needs, you can increase the chances of converting prospects into customers and driving profitability for your business.

Here are some examples of great service business offers and the pain points they solve:

1. Social Media Management: an offer for businesses struggling to effectively manage their social media presence. It includes creating engaging content, scheduling posts, responding to comments, and analyzing performance. By outsourcing social media management, businesses can save time, improve their online presence, and connect with their target audience more effectively.

2. Website Design and Development: an offer for businesses that lack an attractive and functional website. It includes designing a visually appealing and user-friendly website that represents the brand, optimizing it for search engines, and ensuring it is mobile-responsive. This helps businesses establish a professional online presence, attract more traffic, and convert visitors into customers.

3. Virtual Assistance Services: an offer for entrepreneurs and small business owners overwhelmed with administrative tasks. Virtual assistants provide support with email management, scheduling, research, data entry, and other tasks. By outsourcing administrative work, business owners can focus on core activities, increase productivity, and reduce stress.

4. Content Writing and Copywriting Services: an offer for businesses that struggle with creating engaging and persuasive content. It includes writing blog posts, articles, website copy, social media content, and email newsletters. Professional content writing helps businesses attract and engage their target audience, improve their search engine rankings, and increase conversions.

5. **Business Coaching and Consulting**: An offer for individuals or businesses facing challenges in their operations, strategies, or growth. Provide guidance, expertise, and accountability to help clients overcome obstacles, develop effective strategies, and achieve their goals. This addresses the pain point of feeling stuck or lacking clarity in business, providing valuable insights and support for growth.

Pricing Strategies for Service Businesses

Before we delve into pricing, let me share a quick story. I recall a client call where we engaged in conversation to understand each other. They were an excellent fit, and everything went smoothly. When it was time to discuss the investment, I did so. They asked me to send the proposal and assured me they would review it. However, the next day, they reached out to express that they wouldn't be moving forward. The reason? They found my price too low and felt that I lacked expertise.

You see, in the realm of pricing, servicepreneurs often undervalue themselves. This might stem from a lack of confidence in their offering or doubts about their ability to deliver results. These limiting beliefs hold servicepreneurs back, but none of them hold true.

What is true, however, is that as a servicepreneur, you must command premium prices. It's much easier to sell a service for

$2K, $5K, or even $10K than it is to sell a service for $200 or $300. When you sell a high-ticket service, you exude authority. Prospective clients view you as a trustworthy individual. Consider someone trying to sell you a Mercedes S-class or a Rolls Royce for $50K. Quite an unconventional sight, isn't it?

Selling high-ticket services facilitates the attainment of your income goals. Let's say your objective is to earn $10K monthly from your service business. What's simpler: selling your service to 5 clients at $2K each or to 20 clients at $500 each? The answer is clear. By commanding premium prices, you establish yourself as an expert in your field and attract clients who genuinely value and respect your expertise. This not only heightens your perceived value and credibility, but it also streamlines the achievement of your income goals with fewer clients.

Thus, as you shape your pricing strategy, remember to possess confidence in the value you bring and the outcomes you can deliver. Do not underestimate your worth or the worth of your services. Instead, price them in alignment with their true value and the benefits they offer your clients.

Keep in mind that pricing isn't a one-time decision; it's a continuous process. Regularly assess and adjust your pricing strategy based on market dynamics, customer feedback, and the ongoing value you provide. This approach enables you to optimize profitability and maintain competitiveness in the market. So, proceed to set your prices confidently based on the value you provide. As a servicepreneur, you deserve fair compensation for your expertise and the impact you create in the lives or businesses of your clients.

Delivering the Service

After selecting a service business idea, identifying the target audience, and establishing expertise in a specific area, the next step is to determine the service delivery model. This decision is crucial as it will impact the customer experience and ultimately contribute to the success and profitability of the business.

When considering the service delivery model, there are a few options to consider based on the chosen high-ticket price strategy. One option is to offer a "Done For You" (DFY) service. In this model, the service provider takes full responsibility for delivering the service to the client. This could involve handling all aspects of the service from start to finish, without requiring significant involvement from the client. The DFY model provides convenience for clients who prefer a hands-off approach and are willing to pay a premium for a comprehensive solution.

Another option is to offer a "Done with You" (DWY) service. In this model, the service provider works alongside the client and provides guidance and support throughout the process. The client remains actively involved and participates in the service delivery, learning and implementing alongside the service provider. The DWY model is particularly suitable when clients want to be more engaged in the service and desire a collaborative experience.

Alternatively, a hybrid model can be considered. This involves combining elements of both DFY and DWY services. The hybrid model allows for flexibility in catering to different client preferences and needs. Some parts of the service can be delivered as a DFY solution, while other aspects can be done in a DWY format. This approach provides a balanced approach and can accommodate a wider range of client requirements.

Ultimately, the choice of the service delivery model should align with the target audience's preferences and the nature of the service being offered. Conducting market research and understanding customer preferences will help inform the decision-making process. It may also be beneficial to seek feedback from potential clients to determine which service delivery model would provide the most value and meet their expectations.

Remember, the service delivery model can be adjusted and refined over time based on feedback and market trends. It's essential to remain agile and adaptable to continuously improve the customer experience and stay ahead of the competition. Regular evaluation of the service delivery model is necessary to ensure it remains effective and aligned with the evolving needs of the target audience.

By carefully selecting the most suitable service delivery model (whether it's DFY, DWY, or a hybrid), service businesses can create a differentiated offering, enhance the customer experience, and maximize profitability.

Don't Get Screwed Over: Importance of Having Agreements in Place

When it comes to service-based businesses, ensuring mutual understanding and protection is of paramount importance. Regardless of how well-acquainted you are with the client, establishing a formal agreement is a critical step to sidestep potential misunderstandings and conflicts. This agreement should be endorsed by both the client and the service provider, meticulously elucidating the scope of work, deliverables, and the agreed-upon payment terms.

A written agreement not only serves as a tangible reference but also lays a sturdy groundwork for the business relationship, expertly managing expectations. It acts as a safeguard that ensures all stakeholders comprehend their rights and responsibilities, thereby diminishing the likelihood of future disputes or dissatisfaction.

Crafting the agreement necessitates a lucid definition of the scope of work, articulating tasks, deadlines, and any pertinent particulars. This preemptively eradicates any ambiguity concerning the service provider's obligations and the deliverables the client is entitled to receive.

Moreover, the agreement should comprehensively outline the payment terms. It must specify whether remuneration will transpire on a one-time or monthly basis. Inclusion of the agreed-upon financial figure is essential, as are any provisions about late payments, penalties, or potential ancillary expenses. By meticulously delineating these financial terms, both parties preemptively avert potential uncomfortable dialogues regarding monetary matters.

Beyond its immediate utilitarian benefits, a signed agreement furnishes legal shelter to both parties involved. In the event of disputes or breaches of contract, the agreement functions as tangible proof of the prearranged terms and may form the foundation for amicably or legally resolving the predicament.

Undoubtedly, erring on the side of caution proves wiser than being caught unprepared. Regardless of the perceived trustworthiness or reliability of the client, instituting an agreement is a professional protocol that can extricate you from unnecessary complexities and fortify your interests. Hence, before embarking on any service-based business venture, it is judicious to ensure the existence of a well-documented agreement. This document should vividly delineate the scope of work, delineate payment terms, and bear the signatures of all involved parties.

Such diligence not only underscores your professionalism but also secures a solid foundation for a successful collaboration.

Building Relationships Over Profits: The Power of Exceeding Client Expectations

In the world of service entrepreneurship, it is vital to prioritize building strong relationships with clients over focusing solely on profits. Going above and beyond for clients, whether it's the first or twentieth client, can have a lasting and positive impact on your business.

When you prioritize client satisfaction and consistently exceed their expectations, you are more likely to create happy clients who become your biggest advocates. These satisfied clients will not only continue to seek your services but also enthusiastically refer others to your business. Word-of-mouth referrals from satisfied clients can be one of the most effective and cost-efficient ways to grow your business and establish a solid reputation in the industry.

On the other hand, a dissatisfied client can have a detrimental impact on your business. Negative feedback spreads quickly, and one unhappy client can tarnish your reputation and hinder your chances of acquiring new clients. Therefore, it is crucial to prioritize client satisfaction and avoid any disappointments or negative experiences.

To ensure client satisfaction and exceed their expectations, it is important to consistently deliver high-quality services. Strive to provide exceptional value and personalized experiences that make clients feel valued and appreciated. This could involve proactive communication, prompt issue resolution, and going the extra mile to understand and meet their unique needs.

Listening to clients and understanding their goals and concerns is also key to building strong relationships. Regular communication allows you to stay updated on their evolving needs and preferences, helping you tailor your services to better suit their requirements. By actively listening and responding to client feedback, you demonstrate that their satisfaction and success are your top priorities.

Remember that building relationships is an ongoing process. It's not just about impressing clients during the initial stages of the business relationship; it's about maintaining that level of excellence throughout your interactions. Consistency and reliability are crucial in fostering trust and loyalty with clients.

By prioritizing relationships over profits, you create a customer-centric approach that sets you apart from competitors. Your clients will appreciate the personalized attention and exceptional service, leading to long-lasting partnerships and repeat business.

In summary, prioritizing client satisfaction and building strong relationships is vital for the success of your service-based business. Exceeding client expectations not only leads to happy clients who become your loyal advocates but also safeguards your reputation from potential negative feedback. By consistently delivering high-quality services, actively listening to clients, and going the extra mile, you can foster long-term relationships that go beyond profits and contribute to the sustainable growth of your business.

Marketing and promoting you service business.

Crafting Your Digital Image

In the bustling world of service entrepreneurship, where success hinges on connecting with clients and delivering value, one fundamental truth reigns supreme: your online presence can make or break your business before you even get started. In a digital landscape saturated with information and first impressions formed in a matter of seconds, servicepreneurs must master the art of presenting themselves as consummate professionals on social media platforms.

Gone are the days when the process of securing clients was confined to traditional networking events and word-of-mouth referrals. Today, the internet serves as a powerful gateway through which potential clients explore the legitimacy, credibility, and reliability of service providers. And so, before embarking on the journey to secure clients, servicepreneurs are advised to embark on a different journey – one of virtual self-refinement.

Picture this: You're a servicepreneur, eager to transform your passion into a thriving business. You've mastered your craft, honed your skills, and built an arsenal of solutions to cater to your clients' needs. But in the realm of the digital age, the success of your business is intrinsically linked to how well you manage your online presence.

In a world where social media profiles are the modern-day storefronts, potential clients are more likely to click on your profile before they click on your services. Before they even reach out to you, they'll scan your photos, parse your comments, and dissect your interactions. They'll seek to uncover the essence of your character, the extent of your professionalism, and the authenticity of your offerings.

Imagine a prospect looking up your name, only to stumble upon photos of wild parties, crude comments, and questionable behavior. In an instant, your expertise takes a backseat, overshadowed by doubt and skepticism. It's not about suppressing your individuality; it's about presenting a polished version of yourself that aligns with the values of your potential clients.

Hence, the first step in the journey to acquiring clients begins with the transformation of your social media presence. Wipe away any traces of content that could compromise your professional image. Say goodbye to images that are inappropriate or unbecoming of the servicepreneur you aspire to be. Your online persona should reflect the expertise and respectability you bring to your craft.

Moreover, a pristine social media profile is just the beginning. As a servicepreneur, you should curate a compelling narrative through images and words – a narrative that showcases your offerings, encapsulates your value proposition, and provides a direct path for potential clients to connect with you. A profile picture that exudes confidence and approachability, a banner image that highlights your services, and a clear call-to-action that leads to booking a call are crucial components of this narrative.

In this digital age, your social media presence is your handshake, your elevator pitch, and your initial consultation all rolled into one. It's the bridge between your expertise and your clients' needs. So, before you take that leap to secure clients, pause, and dedicate the time to revamp your online persona. Craft a narrative that speaks volumes about your professionalism, value, and commitment to excellence. For in the realm of service entrepreneurship, the first impression is not just the introduction – it's the foundation upon which successful partnerships are built.

Getting your first few clients.

Alright, so you've polished up your online image and you're eager to plunge into the servicepreneur world. But here's the scoop—landing those initial clients? Far simpler than you might be imagining. Seriously, let's skip the complications and delve into the nitty-gritty.

Have you ever heard that sage piece of advice from my mentor? "Closed mouths don't get fed." It's like a little nugget of wisdom you'd find in a fortune cookie, but it's worth its weight in gold. If people aren't aware of what you're all about or how they can support you, well, they won't!

Here's how you can ensure you snag your first few clients as a fledgling servicepreneur:

First off - Get a notepad and scribble down a list of around 20 to 30 individuals you know—your buddies, colleagues, your aunt's dog's walker. You get the drift. These individuals are your golden ticket to those initial clients. Now, let's have a chat about emails. There's no need to craft a novel. Fire off a friendly email or text letting them know you've embarked on a new venture, and that they've been on your mind. Ask for a quick 5-minute chat to discuss your new endeavor and the potential for collaboration. Keep it personal, keep it genuine.

As you tap that "send" button, get ready for a little magic. Replies will start popping up, and you'll be grinning like a kid in a candy store. People adore the personal touch and authentic vibes. Those brief chats will evolve into real connections and—voilà!—potential clients.

Secondly – let's sprinkle some social media fairy dust. I call this the "catch-up moment." Choose your preferred platform—Instagram, Facebook, TikTok, you name it. Go live and have a good old-fashioned catch-up session with your friends using this script: "Hey everyone, it's been a while since I last went live, and today I wanted to hop on here and catch up with all of you. Lately, many of you have been curious about what I'm up to, so I figured I'd come on here and fill you in."

And now, for the grand reveal.

Transition into discussing your brand-new venture. Keep it laid-back, present your offerings, and explain how you can make problems disappear. Then, drop the bomb—invite them to slide into your DMs with any questions or if they know someone who's a perfect fit for your offerings. Encourage them to let you know.

The two strategies I've outlined here are exactly what I used to secure my initial clients and propel my service business to $10k per month within 90 days.

If I managed it, you can too!

Now go out there and make it all happen! I'm firmly in your corner, cheering you on.

Content Reigns Supreme: Creating an Engaging Digital Presence

Picture this: a potential client eagerly hops onto your social media profile to learn more about your service. But what they find is disheartening—a barren wasteland of posts and virtually zero content. Ouch! There's no denying that nothing can turn away a prospective client faster than an empty feed. So, let's talk about why content truly rules the roost, and how you can make it work wonders for your servicepreneur journey.

First things first, content is your ticket to showcasing your expertise and connecting with your audience. It's like your digital megaphone, shouting out what you're all about. But here's the twist—it's not just about throwing information at people. It's about creating valuable, relatable, and engaging content that speaks to both your services and the needs of your audience.

Imagine this scenario: You're scrolling through your favorite social media platform. What grabs your attention? It's not just endless sales pitches, that's for sure. It's content that resonates with you, content that feels like a conversation. That's the kind of content you need to create.

Content creation isn't just a trendy buzzword; it's a powerful tool. When you craft content, you're practicing the art of inbound marketing. You're sharing helpful, free information that pulls potential customers toward your digital doorstep. And don't forget the folks who are already on your bandwagon—you're keeping them engaged and excited by delivering quality interaction.

So, what kind of content should you be whipping up? Let's dive into some creative content ideas that can make your profile a hub of engagement:

Answer a Question: Identify common questions your audience might have and provide detailed answers.

Compare and Contrast Solutions: Help your audience navigate choices by breaking down solutions to common problems.

Teach Something: Offer quick tutorials, how-tos, or mini-lessons that showcase your expertise.

Daily, Monthly, or Weekly Series: Create a consistent series of posts that keeps your audience coming back for more.

Quizzes and Surveys: Engage your audience with interactive content that piques their curiosity.

Curated Content: Share valuable resources from other trusted sources within your industry.

Celebrate Wins: Highlight your successes and those of your clients to build trust and credibility.

Thought Leadership: Share your insights and opinions on industry trends to establish yourself as an expert.

Interview Influencers: Conduct interviews with industry influencers to bring fresh perspectives to your audience.

Discuss Trends: Keep your audience informed about the latest trends and developments in your field.

Contests and Giveaways: Spark excitement and engagement by offering rewards to your audience.

Animate Hard-To-Understand Ideas: Use visuals, animations, or infographics to simplify complex concepts.

Repurpose Blog Content: Turn your blog posts into bite-sized social media nuggets.

How-tos and Tutorials: Offer step-by-step guides for solving specific problems.

Visual Storytelling: Use images and videos to tell a story that resonates with your audience.

User-Generated Content: Encourage your customers to share their experiences and stories.

Infographics: Break down complex information into visually appealing graphics.

Go Behind the Scenes: Offer a sneak peek into your daily operations or creative process.

eBooks or White Papers: Provide in-depth resources that position you as an authority in your field.

Tools and Templates: Offer free resources that your audience can use, building goodwill.

Kits and Workbooks: Create comprehensive guides that walk your audience through a process.

The bottom line is this: content is your golden opportunity to connect, educate, entertain, and engage. It's not just about talking at your audience—it's about crafting a conversation, building relationships, and showcasing your unique value. So, jump on the content train, experiment with different formats, and watch as your online presence flourishes like never before.

The Power of Partnerships, Professional Networks, and Press for Client Acquisition

Client acquisition isn't just a solo act—it's a symphony of collaborations, networking, and strategic moves that can elevate your servicepreneur journey to new heights. In this chapter, we'll delve into the dynamic trio of partnerships, professional groups, and press and how they can work wonders in bringing clients knocking at your virtual door.

Unleashing the Potential of Partnerships:

Partnerships are like a secret sauce for business growth. When you team up with the right players, the impact can be game-changing. Think about it: you're tapping into a whole new audience that's already aligned with your partners' values. Whether it's a fellow servicepreneur, a complementary business, or even an influencer, partnerships can open doors that you might not have access to otherwise.

Imagine combining forces with a business that offers something that complements your services. You're creating a win-win scenario. You get exposure to their clients, and they get access to your audience. It's a handshake that can lead to fruitful collaborations, shared promotions, and ultimately, new clients knocking at your digital doorstep.

Networking Magic in Professional Groups:

If you're looking to amp up your client acquisition game, professional groups are your golden ticket. These groups—whether they're on social media, local meetups, or industry-specific associations—are hubs of like-minded individuals with similar goals. It's like a treasure trove of potential clients just waiting to be tapped into.

By participating in these groups, you're not only expanding your network but also showcasing your expertise and building your reputation. Engage in discussions, share valuable insights, and answer questions—all of which help you stand out as an authority in your field. As you become a trusted voice, potential clients start taking notice. They see you as someone who knows their stuff and can provide solutions to their problems. That's the magic of networking.

Press: Elevating Your Credibility:

When it comes to client acquisition, press coverage isn't just a badge of honor—it's a passport to a broader audience. Getting featured in media outlets, blogs, podcasts, and even local news can boost your credibility and put your name on the map. People tend to trust businesses that have received press coverage; it's like a stamp of approval from experts and journalists.

Landing press coverage isn't reserved for the Elon Musks of the world. Start by crafting compelling press releases about your accomplishments, milestones, or unique offerings. Reach out to journalists, bloggers, and podcast hosts who cover your industry. Share your story, your expertise, and your journey. When you're featured, you not only gain exposure but also attract potential clients who are drawn to your credibility and experience.

When you integrate partnerships, professional groups, and press into your client acquisition strategy, you're creating a multi-dimensional approach that goes beyond the digital realm. By collaborating, networking, and showcasing your expertise in the media, you're opening doors to a whole new world of potential clients who are not just interested but eager to work with you. It's about time you harnessed the power of these three pillars to accelerate your servicepreneur journey.

The Art of Selling Services

The art of selling services is a complex endeavor that involves a deep understanding of customer needs, effective communication, and the ability to convey value. Unlike tangible products, services are intangible offerings that provide solutions, expertise, and experiences. This chapter explores the intricate strategies that define the art of selling services and unveil the techniques that differentiate successful servicepreneurs.

At the core of effective service selling lies a comprehensive grasp of customer needs. This begins with active listening—a vital skill that enables you to decode pain points, aspirations, and goals. By delving into the nuances of each client's situation, you can tailor solutions that address their unique challenges. For instance, a digital marketing agency can tailor its services based on a client's target audience, industry specifics, and distinct marketing objectives.

PETERSON HERARD

Conveying the intrinsic value of services involves strategic storytelling. Unlike tangible products, the value of services often lies in intangible outcomes. Through compelling narratives, you can vividly illustrate the transformative results your offerings deliver. Sharing success stories and case studies serves as a canvas to not only showcase your expertise but also underscore the concrete impact you can make.

Trust-building stands as a pivotal pillar in the realm of service selling. This journey spans multiple interactions, demanding consistent effort. Demonstrating expertise through thought leadership fosters credibility and establishes you as a knowledgeable authority. Transparency in pricing and operations builds trust by assuring potential clients that there are no hidden agendas.

Addressing objections effectively is a crucial component of the service selling process. Treating objections as opportunities for clarity demonstrates your willingness to engage and your commitment to addressing concerns. Articulating responses with nuance and insight can significantly influence potential clients' decision-making trajectories.

Transitioning seamlessly from inquiry to a closed deal requires confidence. Confidently asking for the sale and articulating the value proposition succinctly are key. Coupling this with a touch of urgency, perhaps through limited time offers or exclusive deals, can nudge potential clients toward timely decisions.

The art of selling services is a delicate balance of empathy, adaptability, and conviction. By understanding customer needs, articulating value, establishing trust, and confidently navigating the sales journey, servicepreneurs orchestrate success in an ever-evolving marketplace.

Turning Leads into Loyal Clients

Let's dive into the exciting journey of transforming leads into loyal clients – a process that's not just about business, but about nurturing relationships, delivering consistent value, and embracing their success as your own. In this chapter, we'll uncover the strategic roadmap that savvy servicepreneurs follow to build enduring connections, surpass expectations, and establish unshakeable client loyalty.

At the heart of the art of turning leads into loyal clients is the creation of meaningful relationships. This goes beyond mere transactions – it's about forming authentic connections that resonate. Each touchpoint is an opportunity to establish rapport and trust. Imagine meeting someone new at a gathering – you want to make a genuine connection that leaves a positive impression.

Personalization is the key that unlocks these connections. Tailoring your approach to reflect the unique preferences and needs of every lead show that you're not just interested in their business, but in understanding and meeting their distinct requirements. It's like remembering a friend's favorite coffee order – it shows you care about the details that matter to them.

But that's just the beginning. Exceptional service is the cornerstone that keeps these relationships flourishing. Consistent communication acts as a bridge, keeping clients engaged and aware of the value you provide. Going above and beyond their expectations is like adding an unexpected twist to their favorite recipe – it creates delight and keeps them coming back for more.

Flexibility is your secret weapon in this dynamic journey. Adapting to their changing needs and preferences demonstrates that you're not just a service provider, but a partner in their growth. It's like being the friend who's always up for trying a new restaurant because you know they love exploring new places.

However, it's not just about the present moment – it's about the long-term success of your clients. Proactively recommending additional services or enhancements speaks volumes about your commitment to their growth. It's like suggesting a dessert to complement their meal – you're showing that you're invested in making their experience even better.

Just as a harmonious refrain weave through a song, feedback plays a pivotal role in this process. Seeking feedback isn't just a formality – it's an opportunity to gain insights into their perspectives, preferences, and areas of improvement. It's like fine-tuning your musical performance based on the audience's reactions – it's about continuous refinement to create an even better experience.

The journey of turning leads into loyal clients is a symphony of personalization, exceptional service, adaptability, proactive recommendations, and feedback incorporation. By mastering these elements, you're crafting a narrative of trust, value, and mutual success that not only retains clients but transforms them into fervent advocates of your services.

Unveiling the Advertising Game: Strategic Insights for Servicepreneurs

When it comes to running ads to attract clients, the digital landscape can seem like a vast frontier of opportunity. But here's the twist: my take on the matter leans toward caution and strategic timing. As a seasoned servicepreneur, I firmly believe in a specific milestone before hitting that "run ads" button—a milestone that can make all the difference between a smart investment and a costly experiment. Let's dive into why waiting until you've reached the $20k to $30k monthly revenue mark organically can be a game-changer for your business.

The Sweet Spot: Striking Balance Between Caution and Ambition:

Before you dive headfirst into running ads, it's crucial to establish a solid foundation for your business. Your ultimate goal is to not just survive but thrive, and that requires a careful balancing act between ambition and practicality. Setting a benchmark of $20k to $30k in monthly revenue is a smart move for two key reasons:

Financial Stability: The path to servicepreneur success isn't an overnight sprint—it's a marathon. Running ads without a steady stream of organic revenue can be financially draining, especially if you're yet to establish a solid client base. Hitting the $20k to $30k mark organically provides a cushion that allows you to invest in ads without putting your business at risk.

Feedback and Refinement: Think of your first $20k to $30k in revenue as your playground for improvement. By serving clients organically, you're collecting invaluable feedback that can help you refine your service, iron out any wrinkles, and structure your offerings more effectively. This way, when you do decide to scale through advertising, you're armed with insights that make your campaigns more impactful.

The Power of Data and Iteration:

When you've reached that revenue milestone, you're not just in the financial green zone—you're in a data-rich zone. You've interacted with clients, you've received feedback, and you've tweaked your strategies based on real-world insights. This knowledge is gold when it comes to crafting advertising campaigns that resonate with your target audience.

Advertising without a solid understanding of what works can lead to costly trial and error. With $20k to $30k per month under your belt, you've had enough client interaction to identify pain points, preferences, and patterns. Armed with this data, your advertising efforts become a calculated endeavor rather than a shot in the dark.

Smart Scaling: Beyond the Ads Button:

Reaching that $20k to $30k milestone isn't just about greenlighting ads—it's about setting the stage for smart scaling. It's about leveraging the power of advertising to amplify your existing strengths and refine your weaknesses. With a solid client base and insights to guide you, your ads can hit the bullseye, attracting quality leads that are more likely to convert.

So, take a deep breath and let this sink in. Waiting until you've organically reached the $20k to $30k monthly revenue mark isn't just a cautious approach—it's a strategic one. It's a move that safeguards your financial health while empowering you with the data and knowledge needed to maximize the impact of your advertising efforts.

Remember, as a servicepreneur, your journey isn't a sprint—it's a purposeful stride toward lasting success. And by timing your ads just right, you're not just running a campaign; you're launching an orchestrated symphony of growth that's backed by real results and real insights.

Testimonials: Turning Happy Clients into Your Best Marketing Tool

In the world of servicepreneurship, where trust and credibility reign supreme, testimonials are like gold nuggets that can transform your business landscape. They're not just nice words from satisfied clients; they're potent tools that speak volumes about your expertise, reliability, and the value you bring to the table. Let's dive into the art of testimonials and how they can become your most persuasive marketing asset.

The Testimonial Effect: Building Trust Brick by Brick:

When a potential client stumbles upon your website or social media profile, what's one of the first things they look for? Testimonials. Why? Because testimonials are the social proof that your services aren't just a shot in the dark—they're a tried-and-true solution that others have already benefited from.

Think about it: when someone vouches for your services, they're essentially saying, "Hey, I've been where you are, and I've seen amazing results." It's a powerful endorsement that helps prospects cross the trust barrier and take a step closer to working with you. Testimonials build credibility, and credibility builds trust. It's a chain reaction that can set the stage for a positive client relationship.

The Anatomy of an Effective Testimonial:

Not all testimonials are created equal. To make them truly impactful, there are a few key ingredients to consider:

Specificity: A generic "They're great!" won't cut it. Effective testimonials dive into specifics—details about the problem the client faced, the solution you provided, and the tangible results they achieved.

Transformation: Highlight the transformation your client experienced after working with you. Did they increase revenue? Save time? Gain clarity? Share the before-and-after story to showcase the real value of your service.

Emotion: Let emotions shine through. If your client is genuinely excited about the outcome, let it come across in their testimonial. Emotion resonates with potential clients on a personal level.

Relatability: The best testimonials are relatable. Readers should be able to see themselves in your client's story and imagine how your services could benefit them too.

Authenticity: Authenticity is key. Testimonials that sound too scripted or overly polished can raise skepticism. Let your clients' voices shine through.

The Collection Process: Making Testimonials a Part of Your Routine:

Collecting testimonials should be an ongoing practice rather than a one-time event. Here's how you can make it a seamless part of your client interaction:

Timing: Ask for a testimonial when your client has experienced significant results and is still riding the wave of enthusiasm.

Ease: Make the process effortless for your clients. Send them a simple form or questionnaire to fill out, making it easy for them to share their experience. It's always best to ask for a video testimonial.

Open-Ended Questions: Rather than asking for a general testimonial, ask open-ended questions that encourage your clients to share their journey, challenges, and successes.

Permission: Always ask for permission before using a client's testimonial. Respect their privacy and their right to choose how their words are shared.

Variety: Aim for a variety of testimonials that highlight different aspects of your services. This gives potential clients a well-rounded view of what you offer.

Putting Testimonials into Action:

Once you've gathered a collection of impactful testimonials, it's time to put them to work:

Website: Feature testimonials prominently on your website, especially on pages where potential clients are likely to land.

Social Media: Share testimonials on your social media platforms, along with eye-catching visuals or graphics.

Collateral Materials: Include testimonials in your marketing materials, presentations, and pitch decks.

Email Campaigns: Incorporate testimonials in your email campaigns to showcase the value you provide.

Case Studies: Expand on testimonials by turning them into case studies that delve into the client's journey in more detail.

In a world saturated with choices, testimonials are your secret weapon for standing out. They're not just about singing your praises; they're about demonstrating your impact and building trust. So, when a potential client lands on your digital doorstep, they're not just seeing your words—they're seeing the real-world proof that your services make a difference.

Scaling and Growing Your Service Business

The Skillsharing Method: Unlocking Growth through Strategic Outsourcing

In the dynamic and ever-evolving landscape of servicepreneurship, one undeniable truth becomes increasingly clear: you can't do it all on your own. As an ambitious entrepreneur seeking to make your mark and build a thriving business, you're faced with a constant balancing act—juggling between client acquisition, service delivery, innovation, and myriad administrative tasks. This is where the Skillsharing Method emerges as a strategic beacon of light—a comprehensive approach to outsourcing and delegating tasks that empowers you to harness your time and talents more efficiently, driving exponential growth while maintaining quality.

Embracing the Power of Leverage:

The essence of the Skillsharing Method lies in the acknowledgment that your unique skills and talents are best spent on activities that drive growth and add tangible value to your business. By handing over tasks that either lie outside your expertise or are time-intensive, you unlock a remarkable opportunity for growth and scalability. Whether it's graphic design, content creation, administrative duties, or technical work, there's a world of skilled freelancers out there ready to bring their expertise to your doorstep.

The Multifaceted Benefits:

At the heart of the Skillsharing Method are a multitude of benefits that reverberate across various dimensions of your business:

Efficiency Amplification: By harnessing the expertise of freelancers, you tap into a wealth of specialized knowledge, resulting in superior quality and efficiency. As you focus on your strengths, your collaborators excel in theirs.

Strategic Focus: Liberated from the shackles of mundane tasks, your attention can be wholeheartedly devoted to the strategic aspects of your business. This includes business development, cultivating client relationships, and conceptualizing innovative offerings.

Quality Assurance: The Skillsharing Method doesn't translate to relinquishing control; it's about strategic oversight. As a project manager, you ensure that the final product aligns seamlessly with your standards and your client's expectations.

Cost-Efficiency at Its Best: Imagine closing a lucrative deal with a client for a website project valued at $3,000. Through skillful outsourcing, you're able to find talented freelancers who can execute the project for just $500. The role of the servicepreneur transforms into that of a masterful conductor, orchestrating the collaboration for optimal results.

Unleashing Scaling Potential: By embracing the art of Skillsharing, you're effectively expanding your capacity without overwhelming yourself. You're able to take on multiple projects simultaneously, thereby unlocking the doors to scalability and increased revenue streams.

Navigating the Skillsharing Landscape:

Incorporating the Skillsharing Method into your business strategy involves strategic navigation:

Needs Assessment: Identify the tasks and projects that can be seamlessly outsourced, keeping a keen eye on the ones that can be fully delegated.

Tapping into Talent: Leverage the plethora of platforms like Upwork.com, Fiverr, and specialized Facebook groups to connect with skilled freelancers whose expertise aligns with your requirements.

Meticulous Vetting and Effective Communication: Thoroughly assess potential collaborators, reviewing their portfolios and engaging in clear and open communication about expectations, timelines, and deliverables.

The Art of Project Management: As a servicepreneur, your role transitions into that of a strategic project manager. You steer the collaboration, ensuring that deadlines are met, quality is maintained, and the project aligns with your client's vision.

Client Satisfaction as the North Star: Throughout the process, your primary focus remains on ensuring that the final output meets or exceeds your client's expectations, cultivating a high level of client satisfaction.

The Evolution of Growth Mindset:

Embracing the Skillsharing Method isn't just a tactical choice—it's a transformative mindset shift. You recognize that your time and expertise are invaluable assets that should be directed toward fostering innovation and business expansion. By strategically outsourcing tasks, whether partially or fully, you're sowing the seeds of personal and business growth. The Skillsharing Method doesn't just empower you to shed tasks; it empowers you to take bold strides towards long-term success as a servicepreneur.

In the grand tapestry of entrepreneurship, the Skillsharing Method isn't just a tool—it's an integral philosophy. It's a declaration that your time is too valuable to be consumed by tasks that others can expertly handle. By embracing the strength of strategic outsourcing, you're not only laying the foundation for business expansion and enhanced client experiences, but also fostering your own journey of transformation and growth. As you navigate this realm, remember it's not about what you're giving away, but about what you're gaining in return—the opportunity to soar to new heights as a skilled, visionary servicepreneur.

Building Your Powerhouse: Knowing When to Hire a Team

As a servicepreneur, your journey is a testament to the power of determination, innovation, and strategic thinking. As your business continues to grow, there comes a pivotal moment when the demands of your expanding clientele, projects, and aspirations reach a crossroads. This is the juncture where considering the addition of a team becomes not just a choice, but a strategic move that can propel your business to new heights. Let's explore the signs that it's time to hire a team and why working with contractors might just be your secret weapon for success.

The indicators: Knowing When the Time is Right:

Your business is thriving, and the workload is steadily increasing. You find yourself stretched thin between managing clients, executing projects, and overseeing operations. The first sign that it's time to hire a team is the feeling that you're reaching your capacity—the point where taking on more tasks starts to compromise the quality of your service.

Another clear indicator is the consistent demand for your services. If your pipeline is consistently full and you find yourself frequently turning down projects due to a lack of bandwidth, it's a telltale sign that the time has come to expand your workforce.

The Power of Contractors:

When considering building a team, there's an important distinction to make working with contractors as opposed to hiring full-time employees (W-2). Why contractors? The benefits are plentiful:

Flexibility: Contractors offer the flexibility to scale your team according to project needs. When projects are abundant, you can engage multiple contractors; during quieter periods, you can scale back.

Expertise on Demand: Contractors bring specialized skills to the table. This expertise can be a valuable addition to your team without the long-term commitment of a full-time employee.

Cost-Efficiency: Engaging contractors eliminates the overhead costs associated with full-time employees, such as benefits and office space.

Diverse Perspectives: Contractors often bring fresh perspectives and ideas from their varied experiences, enriching your team's creative pool.

Project-Specific Talent: For certain projects or specialized tasks, contractors can be a perfect match. You're able to assemble a tailored team for each unique challenge.

The Selection Process: Finding the Right Fit:

When selecting contractors to join your team, ensure you follow a structured process:

Define Roles and Responsibilities: Clearly outline the roles and tasks you're looking to fill. This clarity helps both you and potential contractors understand expectations.

Vet and Interview: Thoroughly vet candidates based on their skills, experience, and cultural fit. Conduct interviews to gauge their alignment with your business ethos.

Communication is Key: Effective communication is paramount. Clearly outline project details, expectations, deadlines, and the scope of work.

Legal Agreements: Have a solid contract in place that outlines terms, deliverables, payment structure, and confidentiality agreements.

Collaboration Tools: Set up collaboration tools to streamline communication and project management, ensuring smooth workflows.

Hiring a team, even if they're contractors, is a significant step that should be guided by a clear purpose. Each addition to your team should align with your business goals and contribute to your overarching vision. As you embark on this journey, remember that building a team is an investment—a strategic move that, when executed thoughtfully, can catalyze your business growth, elevate your service quality, and open doors to new possibilities.

In servicepreneurship, your team is an essential thread that weaves together your dreams and aspirations. By embracing the power of contractors, you're not just building a team; you're forging a pathway to collective success, innovation, and the realization of your entrepreneurial vision.

Navigating Success and Key Performance Indicators

Within the intricate landscape of servicepreneurship, your journey is characterized by your aspirations taking tangible form through strategic execution. With every project undertaken, each client interaction, and every decision made, you find yourself drawing closer to the realization of your carefully defined goals. Yet, in the dynamic world of entrepreneurship, an essential query surfaces: How can you be unequivocally sure that your progress aligns with the right trajectory? This is precisely where the concept of Key Performance Indicators (KPIs) steps onto the stage. These KPIs function as the guiding compass steering you through the complexities of challenges, illuminating the paths of opportunity, and crucially, quantifying your advancement. In this chapter, we delve into the significance of diligently tracking success through the lens of KPIs.

The Essence of KPIs: Carving a Path to Progress

Imagine embarking on a journey without a clear destination in sight. KPIs serve as the immovable landmarks on your map, effectively illuminating the route for your business odyssey. By crafting well-defined KPIs, you're not merely setting objectives; you're intricately mapping the trajectory of your business growth.

The Vital Role of KPIs: Measuring and Adapting

KPIs function as the measuring sticks against which your forward momentum and achievements are evaluated. They provide a tangible framework for assessing the efficacy of your strategies and pinpointing areas that warrant refinement. This meticulous approach grounded in data-driven insights empowers you to make well-informed decisions, ensuring that every stride taken resonates harmoniously with your overarching business goals.

An Exploration of Multifaceted KPIs

Recognize that KPIs are not universally applicable; they shift in response to your business's nature, the industry in which you operate, and the distinctive objectives you pursue. Broadly categorized, here are some common types of KPIs that resonate within the realm of servicepreneurship:

Financial KPIs: Encompassing metrics such as revenue growth, profit margins, and return on investment, these provide a real-time snapshot of your business's fiscal vigor.

Client Satisfaction KPIs: Metrics including client feedback, Net Promoter Score (NPS), and customer retention rates serve as indicators of how effectively you cater to client needs and expectations.

Operational Efficiency KPIs: Reflecting areas like project completion times, resource utilization, and process optimization, these metrics illuminate the efficiency of your operational framework.

Sales and Marketing KPIs: Within this domain, you find KPIs such as lead generation rates, conversion rates, and customer acquisition costs, shedding light on the effectiveness of your sales and marketing endeavors.

Productivity KPIs: These metrics, encompassing team productivity, task completion rates, and project milestones, offer insights into the efficiency and output of your team.

Embarking on the KPI Journey

The journey unfolds with a crystalline definition of your business's objectives. Are you driven by the pursuit of amplified revenue, elevated client satisfaction, or streamlined operations?

Selecting the Right KPIs is the subsequent step, aligned closely with your objectives. It is of paramount importance that your chosen KPIs adhere to the principles of being Specific, Measurable, Achievable, Relevant, and Time-bound (SMART).

Consistently Monitoring your selected KPIs assumes a pivotal role. Keeping a vigilant watch over these indicators stands as a necessity for understanding the trajectory of your business. The frequency of assessment may fluctuate, encompassing weekly, monthly, or even quarterly evaluations based on the essence of the KPI.

Interpreting the Insights gleaned from the amassed data holds intrinsic value. This isn't a mere collection of figures; it forms a lens through which you comprehend your progress. The analysis unveils whether you're making headway towards your goals and highlights areas warranting dedicated focus.

KPIs: Flexible Tools for Progression

Crucially, the flexibility of KPIs and their role in facilitating progress comes to the forefront. These indicators are not etched in stone; rather, they adapt and evolve. With the insights garnered, you're poised to steer your strategies and actions towards alignment with your objectives, even as circumstances morph and evolve.

In servicepreneurship, growth is interwoven with informed choices. The careful monitoring of success through KPIs represents a proactive approach, one that harmonizes your endeavors with your aspirations. KPIs function as the illuminating stars, revealing hidden patterns and nuances in your business. These insights bestow upon you the capacity to refine strategies, amplify service offerings, and pivot as demanded by the dynamic landscape.

As you navigate through the entrepreneurial expedition, KPIs operate as the compass, unwaveringly directing you towards your ultimate destination. The journey of a servicepreneur is characterized by evolution, and in this journey, KPIs stand as steadfast allies, equipping you with insights to make judicious decisions and guide your course towards the zenith of success. Always remember that success is not an endpoint; it's an ongoing odyssey – an odyssey propelled by KPIs and your relentless pursuit of excellence.

Common Challenges Faced by Servicepreneurs

Welcome to the realm of service entrepreneurship, where the journey is rife with challenges that test your mettle and creativity. Every servicepreneur encounters a unique set of hurdles on their path to success. In this chapter, we'll delve deep into these common challenges, equip you with insights, and show you how to navigate them strategically.

1. **Finding the Right Clients**: The quest for the perfect client fit can feel like searching for a needle in a haystack. Identifying clients who align with your services, values, and vision requires a blend of strategic targeting and effective networking. It's about narrowing your focus to attract the clients who truly value what you offer.

2. **Pricing Your Services**: The art of pricing services is akin to solving a complex puzzle. Striking the balance between setting rates that reflect your unique value and staying competitive within the market landscape can be a tricky feat. Navigating the delicate dance between profitability and ensuring that potential clients find your rates reasonable is where strategy comes into play.

3. **Managing Workload**: The life of a servicepreneur often involves juggling multiple projects and catering to diverse client needs. Staying organized, managing deadlines, and delivering consistently impeccable work are skills that need to be honed. Think of it as orchestrating a symphony where each note must align perfectly for the composition to be harmonious.

4. **Marketing and Visibility**: In a world saturated with options, making your mark can be a challenge. Effective marketing strategies, crafting a distinctive brand, and establishing a robust online presence are the stepping stones to being noticed amidst the noise. Think of your marketing efforts as your brand's unique melody that captivates and resonates with your target audience.

5. **Handling Client Expectations**: Clients come with a range of expectations, and it's your responsibility to meet or exceed them. This involves mastering the art of effective communication, managing expectations, and setting clear boundaries. Think of it as maintaining a delicate dance where

you lead with transparency and align your steps to the rhythm of your clients' needs.

6. **Scaling Your Business**: As your business gains traction, the challenge of scaling while maintaining the quality of your offerings becomes real. Developing efficient systems, hiring the right team, and upholding your standards in the face of growth become pivotal. Think of it as crafting a masterpiece that remains true to its essence, even as it reaches new heights.

7. **Dealing with Burnout**: The path of a servicepreneur can be exhilarating, but it also comes with its share of stress. Navigating the fine line between pursuing your passion and avoiding burnout requires an artful balance. Prioritizing self-care, setting boundaries, and recognizing the signs of burnout are all essential components of this delicate dance.

8. **Navigating Financial Uncertainty**: The ebb and flow of income streams and the unpredictability of financial circumstances can be unnerving. Preparing for lean times, creating a robust financial plan, and managing your cash flow wisely are the financial strategies that keep your business steady through both calm and stormy waters.

9. **Staying Current**: Industries evolve rapidly, and staying ahead of the curve is a challenge. Navigating the continuous stream of trends, technological advancements, and market shifts requires a commitment to ongoing learning and adaptation. Think of it as the dance of staying in sync with the changing beats of your industry.

Strategies for Overcoming Business Obstacles

In the dynamic landscape of service entrepreneurship, obstacles aren't roadblocks; they're opportunities for growth and transformation. This chapter unveils actionable strategies that empower you to not just tackle challenges, but to leverage them towards achieving your goals.

1. **Embrace Continuous Learning**: In a world that's constantly evolving, staying curious and hungry for knowledge is your edge. Invest in your professional development, attend workshops, and immerse yourself in learning experiences to remain at the forefront of your field.

2. **Build a Strong Support Network**: The journey of a servicepreneur can be solitary, but it doesn't have to be.

Surround yourself with mentors, peers, and advisors who can offer guidance, insights, and a shoulder to lean on during challenging times.

3. **Streamline Processes**: Efficiency is your ally in overcoming obstacles. Streamline your workflows, automate repetitive tasks, and create systems that not only save time but also minimize stress.

4. **Be Agile**: Adaptability is a superpower. When faced with unexpected challenges or shifting market dynamics, be ready to pivot your strategies. Agility allows you to harness the winds of change in your favor.

5. **Communicate Effectively**: Effective communication is the bridge that helps you overcome misunderstandings and navigate conflicts. Develop strong communication skills, practice active listening, and be transparent in your interactions.

6. **Delegate and Outsource**: Recognize that you can't do everything on your own. Delegate tasks that fall outside your core expertise and consider outsourcing specialized needs. Building a team of experts enhances your collective strength.

7. **Prioritize Self-Care**: Your well-being is a non-negotiable asset. Incorporate self-care practices into your routine, whether it's regular exercise, breaks to recharge, or pursuing hobbies that bring you joy. A healthy you is the foundation of a thriving business.

8. **Set Realistic Goals**: Tackling obstacles is a step-by-step journey. Break down significant challenges into smaller,

manageable goals. Achieving these milestones not only boosts your motivation but also propels you forward toward your larger objectives.

Learning from Setbacks and Failures

Setbacks and failures are not dead ends; they're springboards for growth and learning. This chapter delves deep into the art of embracing setbacks, extracting lessons from failures, and harnessing these experiences to propel your journey forward with renewed vigor.

1. **Embrace the Growth Mindset**: The lens through which you view setbacks can make all the difference. Embrace a growth mindset that reframes setbacks as opportunities for learning, evolution, and personal development.

2. **Analyze and Reflect**: When faced with a setback, pause, and reflect. Dive deep into what went wrong, what could have been done differently, and the underlying lessons that can be gleaned from the experience.

3. **Adapt and Iterate**: Failures provide valuable feedback about what doesn't work. Use this feedback to adapt your strategies, pivot your approach, and iterate toward a more successful outcome.

4. **Seek Feedback**: External perspectives offer fresh insights that can shed light on blind spots. Seek feedback from mentors, clients, and peers who can provide valuable input to help you course correct.

5. **Don't Fear Change**: Failure often necessitates change. Don't shy away from embracing new strategies, reimagining your approach, and letting go of what no longer serves your goals.

6. **Reframe Challenges**: Challenges aren't roadblocks; they're creative problem-solving puzzles. Approach challenges with a mindset that embraces innovative solutions and encourages you to think outside the box.

7. **Celebrate Progress**: Acknowledge and celebrate the small victories that arise from setbacks. Each step forward, no matter how incremental, is a testament to your resilience and dedication.

8. **Maintain Resilience**: Building resilience is akin to constructing a sturdy foundation for your journey. Cultivate a strong mindset that allows you to weather storms, bounce back, and emerge stronger on the other side.

9. **Keep Moving Forward**: Remember that setbacks are a part of the journey, not the destination. Harness the lessons learned, the insights gained, and the growth achieved to propel

yourself forward with renewed determination and a
commitment to continuous improvement.

Embracing Your Role as a Servicepreneur

In the realm of service entrepreneurship, your role as a servicepreneur is the core of your business's identity and impact. It's not just a title; it's an embodiment of your dedication, vision, and the mark you intend to leave on the world of services. In this chapter, we'll delve into the profound significance of embracing this role and the principles that guide you along this fulfilling journey.

Creating an Impact: Your role as a servicepreneur is a platform to create real, tangible impact. Through your offerings, you have the power to transform challenges into solutions, answer unmet needs, and elevate the lives of your clients. It's about recognizing that every service you provide carries the potential to make a difference in the lives of individuals and the larger community.

Crafting Personal Connections: Embrace the art of building connections that transcend transactions. Your role isn't just about delivering services; it's about forming bonds with your clients. These connections are built on trust, authenticity, and understanding. When you view your role as a relationship builder, your services become a way to make meaningful connections that endure.

Navigating the Challenges: Challenges are part of the rhythm of entrepreneurship. Your role involves embracing these challenges with resilience and adaptability. It's about recognizing that setbacks are opportunities for growth, and each obstacle is a chance to refine your strategies, learn, and emerge stronger than before.

A Dance of Passion and Profit: Your role involves a harmonious dance between passion and profit. While your passion fuels your dedication, sustainability is essential for your business's longevity. Embrace the balance between creating services that resonate with your heart and crafting a profitable business model that sustains your journey.

Lifelong Learning: As a servicepreneur, you're a perpetual learner. Embrace the ever-evolving nature of your industry. It's about staying curious, seeking knowledge, and being open to new perspectives. Your role involves continuous growth, as each new lesson enriches your ability to serve effectively.

Legacy in Motion: Your role extends beyond the present moment. It's about realizing that the services you provide are part of a larger legacy. Every impact you create, every relationship you nurture, contributes to a legacy that transcends time. Embrace the responsibility of leaving a positive imprint on the lives you touch.

In the dance of service entrepreneurship, your role is both a leader and a partner. It's about setting the tone for excellence, innovation, and unwavering dedication. Embrace this role with pride and passion, for it's your ticket to not just business success, but to a meaningful journey that leaves an enduring mark.

As we conclude this chapter, remember that your role as a servicepreneur is an ongoing story – a story of connections made, challenges conquered, and impact created. Embrace this story, for it's yours to tell, shape, and evolve as you continue to dance through the world of service entrepreneurship.

Conclusion: Your Journey to Profitable Servicepreneurship

As we arrive at the final notes of this comprehensive journey through the world of servicepreneurship, take a moment to inhale the sense of accomplishment that comes with newfound knowledge, insight, and possibilities. These chapters have not merely offered information; they've woven together a tapestry of guidance, inspiration, and empowerment. This book is more than a manual; it's a catalyst for transformation, a compass directing you toward boundless potential.

My aspiration is that these pages have laid down the foundational knowledge essential for you to confidently embark on your service-based business journey. Whether you're embracing this venture part-time, intermingling it with existing pursuits, or wholeheartedly immersing yourself, internalize the principles and strategies shared here – they are the steppingstones to your success.

But remember, this book isn't meant to gather dust on a shelf. It's a companion on your entrepreneurial expedition, a blueprint to be revisited, adapted, and actualized. Servicepreneurship thrives on action – take a concept, infuse it with your ingenuity, see it in action, refine, and repeat. Your journey unfolds as you repeatedly translate words into action, learning through experience and iterating toward excellence.

In the realm of servicepreneurship, progress is a symphony of bold strides. Every action, no matter how small, contributes to the grand composition of your success story. As you navigate this path, embrace the exhilaration of growth, for every move you make shapes your narrative.

Yet, in the pursuit of success, never overlook the essence of faith. While strategies and skills are integral, the cornerstone is your unwavering faith in yourself and the divine providence that guides your journey. Anchored in faith, you transcend limitations and conquer adversities – for with God, all things are possible.

Before you part from these pages, let my parting wisdom resonate this is not just a book to read but a blueprint to live. Embrace your role as a servicepreneur, for it entails more than the mechanics of business; it signifies the birth of your legacy. Craft it with intention, weave it with resilience, and nurture it with fervor.

As you traverse this path, know you're not alone. There exists a tribe of fellow servicepreneurs, mentors, and supporters, all rooting for your success. Relish the challenges, savor the victories, and perpetually embrace the ethos of learning and progress. Your journey as a servicepreneur is an ever-evolving dance – a choreography of innovation, service, and positive transformation.

May your footsteps resonate with purpose, your vision remains steadfast, and your ripple of impact touch lives far beyond your imagination. As the curtain falls on this book, believe that you have the capacity to shape industries, alter destinies, and change the world through your services.

With profound conviction, I extend my wholehearted wishes for the road ahead. As you forge your path, know that you possess the capacity, determination, and potential to achieve greatness. Your services are more than transactions; they're catalysts of change, instruments of empowerment, and beacons of innovation.

This is your journey – a canvas waiting for your masterpiece. As you embrace your role as a servicepreneur, remember that your journey is a continuous crescendo of growth, learning, and influence. The world is your stage, and you're poised to leave an indelible mark.

May your journey be harmonious, your steps purposeful, and your impact enduring.

With the sincerest of wishes and unwavering belief in your potential,

Peterson Herard.